Purvis

A comedy

Nick Warburton

Samuel French — London
www.samuelfrench-london.co.uk

PURVIS

First performed at the Stephen Joseph Theatre, Scarborough
on 16th June 2006 with the following cast

Purvis   Tim Frances
Rachel   Elaine Claxton

Directed by Tamara Harvey

CHARACTERS

Purvis, indeterminate middle-age
Rachel, some years younger than Purvis

SYNOPSIS OF SCENES

The action of the play takes place in the vestry of St Peter's church

Time — the present

Other plays by Nick Warburton
published by Samuel French Ltd

Dickens' Children
Distracted Globe
Domby-Dom
Don't Blame It on the Boots
The Droitwich Discovery
Easy Stages
Garlic and Lavender
Ghost Writer
The Loophole
Melons at the Parsonage
Not Bobby
Office Song
Receive This Light
Round the World with Class 6
Sour Grapes and Ashes
Zartan

PURVIS

WHAT ARE YOU DOING IN HERE?

The vestry of St Peter's church

The room has a single entrance. There is a notice-board on one wall with quite complicated and business-like rotas, marked with coloured stickers, posted on it. From a rack hang vestments for choir and clergy. On a table are various bits of church paraphernalia — box files, hymn books, candlesticks and so on. There is a chair; also a bin

When the Lights come up Purvis is standing very still by the table. He is a nice, mild man of indeterminate middle-age. At the moment he appears lost and worried, like a boy waiting in the head's study. He is dressed neatly but unfashionably. He wears a tie, a checked shirt, a cardigan and grey slacks with turn-ups, and he holds a flat cap which he is crushing and wringing nervously. He thinks he can hear someone coming so he moves from the centre of the room and stands out of the way next to the rack of vestments. But for the cardigan, he might almost be a continuation of them. Instinctively he puts the cap on and stands still

Rachel comes in and fails to see him. Like Purvis, she is rather timid. She is also carefully dressed. In fact, it's Sunday so she's even smarter than usual. Everything about her is precise and controlled. She carries a small, tidy handbag. At the moment she is frustrated and annoyed because she's been looking for Purvis. Normally she would suppress this anger but now she thinks she's alone

Rachel Well, blow him, then. I did my best.

Behind her, Purvis softly clears his throat. Rachel screams and leaps. Purvis also leaps, frightened by the scream

Rachel ⎫ (*together*) Sorry, sorry!
Purvis ⎭

They regard each other, calming down

I'm sorry, I thought you were expecting me.

Rachel No, no. Well, I was but not in here.

Purvis Oh, I thought you said ...

Rachel I've been looking for you, in fact.

Purvis I've been waiting in here. I thought that's what you said, after the service.

Rachel Oh. Perhaps I said in the vestry, then, did I?

Purvis It was in something or other.

Rachel In a minute?

Purvis Ah ...

Rachel I might've said I'd see you in a minute.

Purvis Ah.

Rachel Then I turned round and you were gone. Well, never mind. We've found each other now. Erm, it's Mr ... ? (*She trails the question*)

He's slow to realize what she means. Eventually he does

Purvis Oh. Purvis. (*He remembers his cap and takes it off*)

Rachel Mr Purvis, yes. I'm Rachel.

Purvis Was it about the collection, Rachel?

Rachel The collection?

Purvis In the service. You asked to see me. I assumed it was about the collection ...

Rachel No, no ...

Purvis There was a bit of palaver, see. I'm really sorry. Did you notice? Because the woman bringing the plate round took her eye off the ball a moment and it went flying. The collection plate. It wasn't actually her fault. She didn't see me.

Rachel No, well, it wasn't that ...

Purvis I was on my knees and I bobbed up at the wrong moment. I think it startled her. I was below the level of the pew ...

Rachel No, not to worry. Mrs Armitage is rather a gentle person and she ... Well, you know.

Purvis Yes. I did wonder. I thought I was in trouble.

Rachel (*surprised*) In trouble?

Purvis Well, I got a bit of a dirty look from the vicar.

Rachel Oh, I'm sure not ...

Purvis I think so. He's a bit forceful like that, I've noticed before. Looks a bit disapproving, a bit, a bit, what's the word? Unapproachable.

Rachel Edward's my husband, actually.

Purvis (*surprised*) Is he?

Rachel Yes.

Purvis You're the vicar's wife?

Rachel Yes.

Purvis Oh, I am sorry. I mean, sorry if I said, you know, about him being ...

Rachel No, that's all right, honestly. In fact, it was Edward who told me to see you.

Purvis (*worried*) Oh.

Rachel Well, asked me to ask you, you know.

Purvis Yes, well, as I say. If there is a shortfall or anything ...

Rachel A shortfall?

Purvis In the collection.

Rachel No, really, Mr Purvis, it's nothing to do with the collection ...

Purvis I did find fifty p in my turn-up ... (*He places a fifty pence piece on the table*)

Rachel No, there's nothing wrong, really. (*Smiling*) We don't actually keep people behind after the services.

Purvis Oh. (*Smiling*) Well, thank goodness for that.

Rachel He just wanted to say hallo, really.

Purvis Hallo?

Rachel Yes. Well, obviously he's not here to say it himself: he had to have a word with Colonel Winstone. That's why he asked me. So I could welcome you to the church, on his behalf.

Purvis Oh. That's nice of him. Perhaps you'll say hallo back when you see him. On my behalf.

Rachel I will, thank you. You're new to the area, aren't you?

Purvis I am, yes. Not long moved in.

Rachel Edward said he'd seen you scuttling off after the services and he thought we ought to at least speak. See if we might draw you into the community.

Purvis Crikey. I didn't know I'd been spotted.

Rachel Oh, yes. We'd both noticed you, as a matter of fact.

Purvis Draw into the community. You mean, like Meals on Wheels or something.

Rachel Oh no. Well, I could look into it, I suppose, if you felt it would help ...

Purvis No, not for me. I meant delivering them.

Rachel Oh, I see. Yes, I am sorry. I didn't mean to imply ... They might find an extra pair of hands useful, I suppose ...

Purvis Yes. (*Beat*) I'd do my best, of course, but it wouldn't be easy.

Rachel No?

Purvis I don't drive, you see.

Rachel No? But I thought ...

Purvis No. I did take the test several times, but there was always some small detail I never got quite right. And different each time, which I always found frustrating. I could do the cooking, if it was straightforward, but I couldn't do the driving.

Rachel It's not actually our responsibility, Meals on Wheels ...

Purvis You were thinking of something else, were you?

Rachel Not necessarily. We just wanted to say ...

Purvis You do do other things?

Rachel (*indicating the notice-board*) Well, yes, we have quite a team, but, really, it was only a friendly hallo ...

Purvis (*going to the notice-board*) Oh, yes, I see. All these jobs. You've pretty well got it covered, by the looks.

Rachel Oh, yes. St Peter's runs like clockwork actually ...

Purvis You know, thinking about it, it wouldn't be a bad idea, having something to do. For me, I mean. Something positive.

Rachel Really?

Purvis A way of meeting people. Mary was always worried about that.

Rachel Mary?

Purvis My wife. Late wife.

Rachel Oh, dear. I am sorry ...

Purvis No, no. You weren't to know. But she was always worried I'd keep to myself, you know, that I wouldn't make the effort. She'd love the idea: me with a job in the church. What did you have in mind?

Rachel (*stumped*) Erm ...

Purvis Because your list here is full. Flowers, readers, finance ...

Rachel (*floundering*) At the moment, I suppose, yes ...

Purvis So was it something not listed?

Rachel Yes. (*Beat*) Health.

Purvis Health?

Rachel And Safety. Health and Safety. To keep an eye on things.

Purvis I see, yes. I didn't know churches had Health and Safety.

Rachel Well, it's coming in, Mr Purvis. From Europe. They're very keen on it over there. It's not actually particularly demanding as a job but it is important.

Purvis Health and Safety. Fancy that. It's not a field I know well.

Rachel You wouldn't really have to. It's mostly common sense.

Purvis What would I have to do?

Rachel Erm ... Well, a bit hard to say, really. Mostly checking things, I think. I could ask Edward to have a word, if you like.

Purvis Would he mind?

Rachel I'm sure not. He'd be happy to. And it's better coming from him. You know, all that technical stuff.

Purvis Oh, well, then.

Rachel Why don't you call in tomorrow, about eleven? I know Edward's free then.

Purvis (*pleased*) Could I?

Rachel Of course.

Purvis Right. Eleven, then. Lovely. (*Laughing*) Fantastic. And I thought I was in for a ticking off. (*Shaking Rachel's hand*) Well, thank you, Rachel, thank you very much.

Rachel No, it's our pleasure. I'm sure you'll make a splendid Health and Safety Officer.

Purvis goes

Rachel's smile fades and she looks worried. What will Edward say?

Music

Black-out

SCENE 2
READY FOR ANYTHING

The same. The next day

The flower arrangers have been in. The table has been cleared to make way for a tallish vase and some piles of greenery

The Lights come up and the music fades

Rachel comes in with a checklist of things Purvis might do. It has been given to her by Edward. She paces and reads it over to herself

Rachel (*reading*) Obstacles in the aisles. Switch off unnecessary lights. Coffee and hygiene. (*Looking up*) Coffee and hygiene? What does that mean?

Purvis comes in. He has his cap on again and is wearing a kind of boiler suit. It's clean and neat and makes him look part space technician and part petrol pump attendant. He carries a clipboard

Rachel turns and sees him. The impression renders her momentarily speechless

Purvis (*cheerfully*) Here we are, then.
Rachel Yes.
Purvis Ready for anything. (*He turns to model his overalls and clipboard, miming acute readiness. In doing so, he almost knocks over the vase, though he doesn't notice he's done this*)
Rachel (*moving the vase out of his reach*) So I see.
Purvis Is the vicar not here yet?

Rachel No.

Purvis Oh. It was today, was it?

Rachel Yes, sorry, Mr Purvis. Edward couldn't make it after all. I'd forgotten he had to drive into town. Which I shouldn't've done really.

Purvis Oh dear. I've got you in trouble.

Rachel No, no ... (*Laughing it off*) Just crossed wires, that's all. Anyway, he's given me a list, asked me to have a word.

Purvis Good-oh.

Rachel So I can show you round the church — behind the scenes, as it were. (*Beat*) I hope you didn't go to too much trouble, Mr Purvis, with the overalls.

Purvis Are they not quite right?

Rachel No, no, they're fine. But it's mostly a matter of checking things. It's not actually physical work.

Purvis Well, these came with my old job. They were more or less waiting for the opportunity.

Rachel Oh, well, then. (*Beat*) What did you do?

Purvis I was in printing. I sometimes say I was in print; you know, to lead people on a bit.

Rachel Lead them on?

Purvis Yes. (*Laughing*) So they might think I was writing a book or something ...

Rachel Oh, I see ...

Purvis To get them going. (*Beat*) Anyway.

Rachel Yes.

Purvis I used to wear them when I went down to the machines, which I did from time to time. Now I keep them for weeding the garden. I mean that's when I wear them.

Rachel (*smiling*) Well, we won't ask you to do anything like that.

Purvis Right. Still, if I do see something that needs doing, I've got the gear, haven't I? I can just get on with it, eh?

Rachel I suppose so.

Purvis Then tick it off. Job done. (*Indicating the greenery*) Like this stuff.

Rachel Yes. Well, no. Mrs Armitage left that there ...

Purvis (*gathering up the greenery*) You can get violent reactions from some of this stuff ...

Rachel I'm not sure she's actually finished with that ...

Purvis (*dumping the greenery in the bin*) You only need the choir brushing past. You could have every third one of them out in a rash or something.

Rachel Well, yes. (*Indicating her list*) Shall we get on?

Purvis Yes. (*He doesn't move. Suddenly he seems downcast and unsure*)

Rachel Is everything all right?

Purvis Yes, yes. Well, I was wondering: is Edward ...? I mean, will the vicar be joining us?

Rachel I'm afraid not. My fault. I shouldn't have booked him in without checking ...

Purvis No, no, fair enough. It's probably easier to tell you anyway.

Rachel Tell me what?

Purvis Well, it's sort of difficult to explain, what with you being so kind and everything ...

Rachel Mr Purvis, what is it?

Purvis The thing is, I'm not too sure about this. In retrospect.

Rachel Oh?

Purvis You know, Health and Safety.

Rachel (*relieved but covering*) Well, we don't want to force you. That's the last thing we want ...

Purvis Trouble is, if there's work to be done ...

Rachel Well, I wouldn't say that ...

Purvis You'll need someone. I'd be letting you down if I backed out now.

Rachel No, no, of course you wouldn't.

Purvis No?

Rachel Of course not.

Purvis You're just saying that.

Rachel No, really ...

Purvis I'd feel responsible. After getting your hopes up.

Rachel No.

Purvis I think I would.

Rachel We'll be fine, honestly. (*Beat*) Have you found something else? Is that it?

Purvis Not really. It's more ... (*Pause*)

Rachel What?

Purvis I'm not sure I'm up to it.

Rachel Oh, Mr Purvis.

Purvis I don't think so.

Rachel Of course you are.

Purvis I sit at the back there, in the service, and I can't help thinking it's all a bit posh for me. How can I tell that lot what to do? They're out of my league ...

Rachel You wouldn't have to tell them what to do.

Purvis I might. I was awake half the night thinking about this. There's an old boy, sits near the front with a walking stick, wears a blazer.

Rachel Colonel Winstone?

Purvis Exactly my point. Colonel, you see. Officer class. How can I go up to a man like that and tell him his stick's poking out?

Rachel (*not quite with this*) His ... ?

Purvis Walking stick. In the aisle. Because that's the kind of thing I'd be looking out for, and I couldn't tell him. I'm not up to it.

Rachel His stick's in the aisle, then, is it? I've never noticed ...

Purvis Well, no, it isn't, but it might be ... He could have an entire procession down — and that's just the kind of thing a Health and Safety Officer ought to point out.

Rachel Well, you could tell me, and I could have a word with Edward, and ——

Purvis He'd know it was me, though. My name would be on the list: Health and Safety — Purvis.

Rachel But if he's in the wrong, if his stick is poking out ...

Purvis Would you tell him, Rachel?

Rachel Me?

Purvis Or suppose it was the vicar. Suppose he leaves a banana skin on the pulpit steps ...

Rachel I don't think that's likely.

Purvis Would you tell him, though? Would you say, "Oi! Don't leave that there. That's a hazard"?

Rachel Well, not like that, no.

Purvis Yes, but you can't delay when it comes to safety. You can't wait for the right moment. Till you're in bed or something, and you can work your way round to it ...

Rachel Of course not. I'd simply mention it.

Purvis You're sure? Because he was a bit short when he asked you to have a word with me, wasn't he? And he didn't like it when you pencilled me in his diary.

Rachel I never said that.

Purvis He didn't, though, did he? So you might be tempted to wait for a better time. And there it stays, festering, the banana skin on the step. And the bishop goes up to preach, and whump!

Rachel I think we've strayed from the point. We're not talking about me. And you would be the Health and Safety *Officer*. You *would* have the authority.

Purvis I don't know ...

Rachel Well, I really don't want to talk you into this if you'd rather not, but, honestly, don't back out because you don't think you'll be up to it, because that's not a very good reason.

Purvis I feel uneasy.

Rachel What would Mary say?

Purvis (*taken aback*) What?

Rachel Your wife. What would she have said?

Purvis Oh. Well ...

Rachel Would she let you back out? She'd have said you were daft to think about it, wouldn't she?

Purvis Well ...

Rachel She would've encouraged you.

Purvis Yes. Yes, she would. A chump. That's what she'd say. "Don't be a chump."

Rachel There you are, then. You don't want her thinking you're a chump, do you?

Purvis considers this. Pause

Purvis I could give it a go, at least.

Rachel Of course you could. And it's mostly common sense, as I said. You'll be fine.

Purvis Yes. A matter of keeping your eyes skinned. I can do that. It's just the telling-people bit.

Rachel They'll take it, if you're firm. And decisive.

Purvis (*trying it out*) "Have you finished with that banana? So where are you going to put it?"

Rachel They'll jump to it, Mr Purvis. (*Beat*) Shall we take a little look round the church?

Purvis Yes, please.

Rachel This way, then. (*She heads off*)

Purvis stops Rachel before she gets as far as the other end of the table

Purvis (*with his new authority*) Just a minute. Shouldn't we start in here?

Rachel In here? (*She checks Edward's list*) Edward didn't actually mention in here ...

Purvis leans against the table, testing it

Purvis Perhaps he should've done. I mean, this isn't as secure as it might be.

Rachel (*smiling*) No. Perhaps you're right.

Purvis Bit of angle-iron fitted to the leg. I could do that myself.

Rachel I have absolutely no doubt.

They smile. Purvis lifts the table to examine the leg. The vase shoots off the end. Rachel manages to catch it. Purvis doesn't notice. He makes a note on his clipboard

Purvis Vestry table — angle iron on table leg. (*To Rachel*) Perhaps you'll mention that to Edward. Right. Let's see what else is lying in store for us, shall we?

Enthused, Purvis marches out

Rachel replaces the vase, looks after him a moment, and then follows

Music

Black-out

The same. Some days later

There are signs of minor disorder in the vestry. For example, the notice-board might be a little crooked and the table more cluttered. A plastic bag and a small tray of make-up, face paints, talcum powder, pots of hair gel and the like, has been set on the table. There is also a roll of paper towel

The Lights come up and the music fades. Purvis is sitting examining the contents of the tray, taking lids off, sniffing things

Rachel comes in carrying items to pin on the notice-board. She's pleased to see Purvis. She sets about pinning the items to the board

Rachel This is getting to be home from home for you, Mr Purvis.

Purvis I know. There's rather a lot to do.

Rachel Yes.

Purvis More than I thought, in fact. I'm not getting in the way, am I? I've more or less taken over this table.

Rachel You're fine. It's nice to see the place used, I always think. There's been some bustle since you joined us. (*She smiles at him*) By the way, Edward said to tell you the photocopier's on the blink. He thought you might know about it.

Purvis Well, yes, I do.

Rachel He was a bit put out actually because not only was it broken, it was absolutely sticky with cold coffee.

Purvis Yes.

Rachel Major nuisance. You do know, then? Edward said you would.

Purvis I was there when it happened. Mr Kavanagh was running off some song sheets as I came through. I sort of clipped his elbow as I passed.

Rachel Oh dear.

Purvis It was always on the cards, something like that, with the machine being near the door. You can't blame Mr Kavanagh.

What it needs, I think, is either to move the photocopier up the other end of the church, by the main door, or make a notice. To warn people that photocopying might be in progress.

Rachel A notice would be best, Mr Purvis, probably. It'd be less intrusive.

Purvis I'll get on to it, then. Tell Edward not to worry.

Rachel Right.

Purvis Does he want me to take a look at the copier?

Rachel No ...

Purvis I could, if he likes.

Rachel No, he's getting the man in.

Purvis I'm very cheap ...

Rachel Thank you, yes, but he got on to it immediately. He's terribly impatient with things going wrong, Edward is. Has to tackle it straight away. Which you can understand in his position.

Purvis At the helm.

Rachel Yes. It's like the cooking.

Purvis Is it?

Rachel Edward does all the cooking. I'm not terribly good at it, you see, and he likes things to be right

Purvis I'm sure you're very good ...

Rachel Not really. I did this thing with sardines and prunes when we were first married and after that he said ——

Purvis Sardines and prunes?

Rachel I didn't know they were prunes. I didn't know what prunes looked like. And they really didn't go well together. Sometimes odd things do go together but these didn't. Edward said it would be best if I left the cooking to him after that.

Purvis Ah, well. Perhaps you'll surprise him one day. (*Smiling*) You haven't got a moment now, have you?

Rachel A moment, yes. Why?

Purvis I want to ask your opinion about something. (*Taking up the plastic bag*) You sure you don't mind?

Rachel I don't mind. Unless you'd rather wait for Edward?

Purvis No, no. I'd value your opinion. Right. I'll be with you in a moment. (*He dives out of sight behind the table with the plastic bag*)

Rachel turns back to her notice-board

Rachel (*calling over her shoulder*) Can I help at all?

Purvis (*from behind the table*) No, thank you. I just want to know what you think. It's a little initiative I've been considering — linked in with the safety issues. (*He emerges. He has put on a piratical black beard and joke teeth and looks startlingly different. He waits to be noticed*)

Rachel I must say it's surprised us all, Mr Purvis. The sheer energy you've found for all this ... (*She turns and sees him. She gasps with shock*)

Purvis What do you think?

Rachel I really don't know ...

Purvis I wondered if it needed a touch of colour. Hence the paints and things.

During the following, he applies dobs of colour to his cheeks

Rachel Safety initiative, did you say?

Purvis Yes. For the kiddies.

Rachel I can't quite see the link.

Purvis Ah. Well, I was remembering when I was at school and Safety Sam ... (*removing the joke teeth*) Safety Sam came round to talk to us about riding bikes and crossing roads and things, and he was really hopeless. (*Laughing*) It was amazing: he got everything wrong ...

Rachel And he was Safety Sam?

Purvis Yes. Or was the sensible one Safety Sam? That would make more sense, wouldn't it? Perhaps the other one was called something else. Anyway, I was thinking I could try something similar with the kiddies from the Sunday School. Teach them about health and safety round the church, but in a light-hearted way. What do you think?

Rachel I'm not sure.

Purvis No?

Rachel I think it might clash with Stranger Danger. We try to discourage them from talking to strangers.

Purvis I wouldn't really be a stranger, though.

Rachel Yes, but you do look a bit, well ...

Purvis What?

Rachel Sinister.

Purvis Oh. Well, we don't want that. Perhaps the make-up will help. You know, tone down the sinister side of things a bit.

Rachel I don't think so. I have to say I don't think Edward will be all that keen either.

Purvis Really? (*He thinks*) You could do it, though.

Rachel Me?

Purvis Yes. The kiddies know you. They wouldn't be scared of you.

Rachel I should hope not, but I'm not sure ...

Purvis puts hair gel on his hands

What're you doing?

Purvis (*moving towards her*) All you'd need is a bit of this stuff to make your hair stick up a bit ...

Rachel (*backing away*) Mr Purvis, no!

Purvis Create an impression, make it more memorable for them ...

Rachel For goodness' sake!

Purvis You know, fun but ——

Rachel (*loudly*) Absolutely not!

Pause. Purvis is frozen, his hands full of gel, looking embarrassed and apologetic. Rachel looks at him and laughs, partly through nerves

You weren't really going to ... Were you?

Purvis I don't know. (*Beat*) Sorry. (*He looks around for somewhere to wipe his hands. There's nowhere*)

Rachel Here, let me. (*She finds the paper towel and wipes his hands*)

He lets her

Purvis I sort of got carried away. I probably overstepped the mark there.

Rachel Slapping hair gel on somebody else's head, Mr Purvis; I
think you probably did.

*Purvis looks sorrowful. Rachel laughs again, more warmly, and
finishes wiping his hands*

Purvis I do get overenthusiastic sometimes. You'd have to tell me.
If I did again at any time. You'd have to be straight with me.
Rachel I will, Mr Purvis. Don't worry about that.

Music

Black-out

SCENE 4
IS THERE A PATTERN?

The same. A day or so later

The place is a little less tidy; things are piled on the chair and table

*The Lights come up and the music fades. Purvis is hammering wildly
at a board which he's attaching to a pole. It is a sign, the words not
yet visible, saying "Mind the Step" in large letters painted by Purvis
himself, with an arrow*

*Rachel comes in to have a word. She calls to him but he doesn't hear
because of the hammering*

Rachel (*calling*) Mr Purvis ...

Purvis still doesn't hear her because of the hammering

Mr Purvis ...

After a moment he stops hammering and, in the quiet:

(*Shouting*) Mr Purvis!
Purvis (*startled*) What? What is it?

Rachel Sorry, sorry ... I didn't mean to ...

Purvis Rachel.

Rachel Yes. Have you got a moment? Or shall I come back?

Purvis No, no. Come in. You want to be careful, though, popping up like that.

Rachel Yes ...

Purvis If you'd caught me at the top of my swing ...

Rachel Well, yes ...

Purvis I dread to think. Mind you, I probably shouldn't be using this table as a workbench.

Rachel No, perhaps not.

Purvis You don't get enough resistance. It really needs putting against something a bit firmer. A few hymn books, perhaps.

Rachel Or the step outside. Against the stone.

Purvis Good point, good point. I might just try that.

Rachel What is it exactly?

Purvis This? It's a sign. (*He holds it up*)

Rachel I see.

Purvis "Mind the step."

Rachel Yes.

Purvis It's for Communion.

Rachel Erm ... ?

Purvis Communion. You know.

She's still blank

Well, they all troop up, roughly in a queue, and they branch off to the right — stage left, as it were, from where Edward's standing — up to the altar rail, two steps, and kneel, see ——

Rachel Yes, but ...

Purvis — and their minds aren't on their feet.

Rachel Well, no, but ...

Purvis No, I've been watching them, Rachel, and they don't concentrate. Perfectly understandable in the circumstances, of course, their attention is elsewhere, but it does render them vulnerable to the sudden pitch forward. (*A small demonstration*) So. (*He indicates his sign*)

Rachel Where would you put it?

Purvis Tack it to the end of the altar rail.

Rachel "Mind the step"?

Purvis Well, when I say tack, I really mean fix a small bracket ...

Rachel No. No, we couldn't. It wouldn't look right ...

Purvis I think you'll find it looks a bit better than someone slumped across the altar rail with a nose bleed...

Rachel No, Mr Purvis, I don't think so. Anyway, it hasn't actually happened, has it? No-one ever has tripped on those steps ...

Purvis They have, you know.

Rachel Well, yes, you have but, but ...

Purvis (*taking mock offence*) Surely you're not suggesting I don't count?

Rachel No, Mr Purvis, I didn't mean that. It's just, well, you're talking about altering the fabric of the church.

Purvis Not necessarily. Someone could stand there holding it, then, during the services. If we had a rota.

Rachel I don't think so ...

Purvis I wouldn't mind doing it.

Rachel Standing there with a pole? You'd look like a lollipop man.

Purvis (*putting the sign down*) You have a chat to Edward about it, then. Will you do that for me?

Rachel Of course.

Purvis See what he thinks, when he's feeling up to it.

Rachel Yes. Yes, perhaps I should do that. (*Smiling*) Actually, Edward's asked me to have a word with you.

Purvis Has he? Poor old Edward. How is he? How's he doing?

Rachel A bit better today, thank you. He's still resting, though.

Purvis What did the doctor say?

Rachel She was rather vague, really. She said he was in reasonable condition physically, but he was suffering some sort of nervous exhaustion.

Purvis He takes things so seriously, doesn't he? That's half the problem.

Rachel Perhaps he does, but he was genuinely distressed by what happened, Mr Purvis.

Purvis Of course he was, of course. It would've given anyone the yips. Still, I'm glad to hear he's a bit better. On the mend, eh?

Rachel Yes ...

Purvis Tell him we all press on in his absence.

Rachel Yes.

Purvis It might be some comfort, to know that. Show him the sign — it might perk him up. Will you do that? Pop the sign in, so he can have a little look?

Rachel Yes.

Purvis You could stand at the end of the bed with it. So when he opens his eyes ...

Rachel Yes, well, we'll see how he is. (*Awkwardly, not wanting to say what she has to*) As a matter of fact ...

Purvis What?

Rachel Well, what Edward wanted me to say ... Because you mentioned everyone pressing on, and things really have been pressing on, haven't they?

Purvis Oh yes, I should say so.

Rachel And what Edward was wondering was whether there was some sort of — well, pattern.

Purvis Pattern?

Rachel Emerging. Whether recent events, here in the church — whether there was a kind of trend …

Purvis You mean illness-wise? Things getting him down?

Rachel Perhaps pointing in that direction, yes.

Purvis What sort of recent events?

Rachel Well, just to take one thing at random, the door to the organ loft for example.

Purvis Ah, that, yes. I'm surprised no-one mentioned that before.

Rachel No-one's said anything to you, then?

Purvis They should've done in my opinion, but they haven't. There was quite a draught coming through that door. It's a self-closing door, you see, and the spring was slack.

Rachel Yes, but ...

Purvis I found a better one. Much more clout.

Rachel Yes. As Mrs Armitage discovered.

Purvis Well, obviously it's going to have a bit of a kick, especially when it's new ——

Rachel The swing rather took her by surprise ...

Purvis — simple mechanics should've told her that ...

Rachel It was lucky she was coming out and not going in. At least
she had a clear run.

Purvis Well, quite.

Rachel Straight down the side aisle.

Purvis Luckily I was there at the time. My word, she came out of
that loft like a greyhound out of a trap. (*Chuckling*) The organist
entertains, eh?

Rachel It's not funny, Mr Purvis.

Purvis No, of course not. But she saw the funny side herself after
a bit of a cuppa. And she wasn't hurt.

Rachel Fortunately.

Purvis Quite.

Rachel Unlike Wellington.

Purvis Wellington?

Rachel The colonel's dog.

Purvis Is that what it's called? That yappy little thing?

Rachel You can't really blame him for yapping ...

Purvis It was the tip of his tail, that's all.

Rachel Even so ...

Purvis I don't know if you were aware of this, Rachel, but that
hedge-trimmer was nearly written off.

Rachel I was aware of it, yes ...

Purvis Just as well it cut out when I dropped it. Otherwise ...

Rachel No-one knew you were tackling the hedge.

Purvis Someone had to. It was becoming a hazard.

Rachel You see what I'm getting at, though. These accidents. First
Mrs Armitage and then Wellington.

Purvis Yes.

Rachel And the photocopier getting doused in hot coffee. Again.

Purvis Again, yes.

Rachel When the lights went out on Mr Kavanagh.

Purvis That was energy saving, of course ...

Rachel And the wedge you put in to stop the lectern wobbling.

Purvis It did wobble a bit, though ...

Rachel Perhaps it did, but it also remained upright, didn't it?

Purvis Well, yes. I'm fairly confident it'll bend back into shape ...

Rachel And then, of course, the ladder to the belfry.

Purvis Oh, d'you think so? I hadn't actually seen that as an accident.

Rachel I think it really does qualify, Mr Purvis.

Purvis Even though I was actually moving it out of harm's way? You know, in case some kiddy ventured up. Which would've been worse.

Rachel Edward was up there six hours. I thought he was in York.

Purvis Dear oh dear, was it as long as that?

Rachel Yes, and it was most disturbing. You could see: he was physically shaking when we got him down.

Purvis He never saw my sign, that's what went wrong there. I made a sign to say the ladder wouldn't be left out and that anyone using it should inform someone else. Preferably me ...

Rachel You weren't there, though, were you? And Edward didn't see the sign because you'd gone home to paint it. There wasn't a sign at the time. So you see the point I'm making? About a pattern emerging?

Purvis (*thoughtfully*) Well, I suppose I do, yes.

Rachel looks at him carefully. She hopes he's not offended

Rachel I hope you don't mind me mentioning it.

Purvis Of course not. You have to, something like this. For all concerned. It's obviously far more dangerous than you thought, this place.

Rachel (*surprised*) This place?

Purvis The church. Both inside and out, I'd say. Probably because it's so old ...

Rachel I don't think it's the church, Mr Purvis.

Purvis That graveyard out there, for example. It's a potential death-trap. You only have to look at it.

Rachel No, I wasn't talking about ...

Purvis In fact, there's health and safety issues all over the shop once you start looking. Thank goodness you asked me when you did, that's all I can say.

Rachel (*firmly*) No, please, Mr Purvis, just listen a moment. It's really nothing to do with the church being old or anything ...

Purvis I think it might be, you know ...

Rachel Just hear me out, please. The church has been old for years so it's not that. I mean, there isn't actually a tradition of people walking into holes which appear overnight. (*Before he can explain*) Yes, I know, I know, the paving stones needed levelling, but suddenly there was a hazard there, wasn't there? Someone removed some of the stones and dug a hole ...

Purvis I did.

Rachel Yes, you did. And it was quite a deep hole, some might say an unnecessarily deep hole, so when someone came round the corner ...

Purvis Edward.

Rachel Yes, Edward as it turned out, but it could've been anyone. This isn't personal, Mr Purvis. You see, what Edward's getting at is that, not to be too blunt about it, we've had this chapter of accidents and we didn't have them before. We were going along quite nicely and then we took on a Health and Safety Officer and suddenly it seems people are being felled left, right and centre. Do you see what I'm getting at?

Purvis I think so.

Rachel In a way I feel responsible ...

Purvis What? Why?

Rachel Well, I encouraged you to become involved ...

Purvis Don't be daft. How is that your fault?

Rachel Yes, but if you are actually accident-prone ... And I'm not saying you can help it ...

Purvis Accident-prone? That's daft, that is.

Rachel It does begin to look like that, though.

Purvis Nonsense. You can't blame yourself ...

Rachel No, I wasn't ...

Purvis No, my turn now. You listen to me. Sit down. (*He tips things off the chair and makes her sit*) You're not accident-prone, Rachel. Get that out of your head. It's just coincidence, that's all. All these little hitches, they've been waiting to happen, probably for years and years. Along you come and you appoint a Health and Safety Officer, and then you get, as you say, a sequence of events, a chapter of accidents. Now how can that be your fault?

Rachel I'm not saying it is ...

Purvis There's no logical link, is there?

Rachel Not in the way you mean ...

Purvis Good. Good girl. You're doing something about it, that's the point. Edward's not happy, though. Is that the problem?

Rachel No, he's not ...

Purvis We can soon put that right. Don't worry about that. I'm working on it on a daily basis. Tell you what, you cook him up something special. That'll take his mind off things.

Rachel No, I don't think I could.

Purvis Course you could.

Rachel No, I told you. Edward does the cooking ...

Purvis Ah yes, sardines and prunes. Well, in that case you can surprise him, can't you? I've got a sure-fire recipe for fishcakes. Never fails. I'll talk you through it.

Rachel Yes but ...

Purvis You'll see. Fishcakes to soothe the savage breast, eh? (*Taking up the sign*) And you can give me a hand with this as well.

Rachel I'm not really blaming myself, Mr Purvis ...

Purvis Excellent. Right, then. Let's get this sign finished. We'll take it outside and you can hold it still while I tap the last couple of nails in. Eh? How about that? That'll cheer you up. Then you can make those fishcakes for that husband of yours, eh? How about that? Will you do that? Will you promise me you'll do that?

Rachel I will, but ...

Purvis Brilliant. Come on, then. Let's get cracking.

Before she can protest, he swings the sign round, knocking books from the table

You take that end.

Rachel takes hold of the end of the sign

Purvis marches out, dragging Rachel behind him

Music

Black-out

The same. Some days later

There are more signs of disorder. There is another flower arrangement on a stand. It looks as if it's been abandoned halfway through

The Lights come up and the music fades. Rachel is pacing anxiously. She has a large bandage on one thumb. From time to time she refers to a postcard, as if she's learning lines

Rachel The thing is ... I mean, it's not actually working terribly well, is it? You only have to look around ... (*Sighing*) The thing is, Mr Purvis ... I think it's probably best all round — best for all concerned ... (*Starting again*) I think maybe I should come straight to the point, Mr Purvis ...

Purvis bursts in. He's enthused by something. Rachel hides the postcard

Purvis Ah, there you are. Colin said you were in here.

Rachel Yes, yes, I am ...

Purvis I just wanted to run something by you, as they say.

Rachel (*looking worried*) Yes, me too. To run by you, that is. Something to say, I mean.

Purvis (*seeing her worried look*) Are you all right?

Rachel Yes, I'm fine ...

Purvis You look a bit peaky ...

Rachel No, really ...

Purvis It's not your thumb, is it?

Rachel No ...

Purvis Because you did go a bit faint, you know.

Rachel I remember.

Purvis It was lucky I was there. Or maybe you've eaten something. Have you, d'you think? Something that's disagreed with you? (*A sudden thought*) Of course. You were on the cake stall, weren't you? At the Spring Fayre?

Rachel Yes, why?

Purvis Well, I had to blow the whistle on Mrs Armitage's banana cake.

Rachel Blow the whistle?

Purvis Kick it into touch. You didn't have any, did you? Before I condemned it?

Rachel No ...

Purvis Thank goodness for that. I can't imagine you would, really.

Rachel You condemned it?

Purvis Well, it was pretty disgusting, poor old dear. God knows what went into it; it looked like plasticine.

Rachel You banned her cake?

Purvis I had to.

Rachel So that's what upset her.

Purvis I shouldn't think so. This was Saturday.

Rachel Well, she's obviously been brooding on it.

Purvis Do you think?

Rachel She hardly spoke a word during matins yesterday.

Purvis Oh dear ...

Rachel And she was in here this morning, doing the flowers, and she suddenly went off in tears.

Purvis Oh dear. I'll have a word with her. Smooth things over.

Rachel Mrs Armitage has always had banana cake in the Spring Fayre.

Purvis You can't be sentimental with diarrhoea and sickness at stake, though, can you? (*Beat*) Anyway, as long as you're well.

Rachel I'm fine, I'm fine. Just, you know, a few things on my mind.

Purvis Anything I can help with?

Rachel Not really.

Purvis You're sure? A problem shared is a problem halved, you know.

Rachel Yes, it can be.

Purvis Well, you know where to find me.

Rachel Yes.

Purvis I'm always here.

Rachel Yes, you are these days, aren't you?

Purvis What did you want? You said you wanted to ask me something.

Rachel (*after a beat*) No, it can wait. After you.

Purvis Sure?

Rachel Please, go ahead.

Purvis I don't want to tread on any toes ...

Rachel (*a little impatiently*) Just tell me. Please.

Purvis Right. (*Pleased*) Well, I thought you'd be interested to know that Colin Cosgrave's asked me to join the Social Committee?

Rachel (*surprised*) Has he?

Purvis He's co-opted me. The others asked him to ask me, apparently. Isn't that nice?

Rachel Well, yes ...

Purvis They said there was a gap now Edward's withdrawn. As a matter of fact, I wondered if you'd had anything to do with it.

Rachel No, I didn't. I didn't even know about it. Edward hasn't said anything.

Purvis No, Edward doesn't know yet. We're going to tell him on Friday.

Rachel What?

Purvis So there's me now on the Social Committee. I can hardly believe it. I never thought of myself as the executive type. Still, it's gone all right so far.

Rachel You mean you've already started?

Purvis Oh yes. I've had a couple of meetings already.

Rachel Have you?

Purvis Oh yes. In fact, I've actually made a contribution. You know what it was?

Rachel No.

Purvis I'll tell you. No, no — I'll show you. And I want you to tell me exactly what you think of this. You know, your honest opinion. (*He stands still for a moment, gathering himself, and then goes into a routine of steps and arm movements. It looks like a dance as done by someone bringing a jet in to land*)

It's not what Rachel was expecting and she's taken aback. It finishes. Pause

Well?

Rachel I'm not sure, Mr Purvis.

Purvis It's basically very simple — easy steps and arm movements ...

Rachel I mean, I don't understand. You suggested this to the Social Committee, did you?

Purvis Yes. It's to go with the hymns. Didn't I say that?

Rachel Hymns?

Purvis Yes.

Rachel No, you didn't. What do you mean, exactly: to go with the hymns?

Purvis To add a little movement. It's an idea I got while I was patching up the lectern the other day. For some reason I was recalling the Black and White Minstrels, you see. You won't remember the Black and White Minstrels, you're too young, but they used to be very popular. Of course, they wouldn't do so well these days because they were racist. Well, maybe not all of them, as individuals, I mean. In fact you weren't always aware of them as individuals because they were blacked up. But the concept was, if you see what I mean. Racist.

Rachel I'm not really following you.

Purvis No, well, forget the racism. That confused the committee as well but it's really nothing to do with it. This is to do with the way they used to sing and dance. Because some of them were getting on a bit. And they were also a bit fat, some of them. So although the younger ones could be fairly nifty and do all the steps, the fat ones just used to shuffle from foot to foot and move their arms. In a way it was sort of democratic — you know, giving the fat ones a fair crack of the whip, making it look as if they were joining in while all the other ones went hurtling by. And then I thought it's a bit like our congregation here at St Peter's. I mean, if you blacked them up ...

Rachel Mr Purvis, you haven't suggested ... ?

Purvis No, no. It's just the movement aspect I'm thinking of. Sort of aerobic hymn singing.

Rachel You mean you want the congregation to jig about ... ?

Purvis I wouldn't call it jigging about. It's more organized than that. Those movements I showed you, see, they can be adapted to almost any hymn you can name. Look.

Purvis repeats the dance, this time singing a burst of "He Who Would Valiant Be" at a lively pace, and then segueing into a slower rendition of "Silent Night" for which he moves more slowly and flowingly. Rachel watches. Purvis's movements threaten the flower arrangement on its stand so at some point she moves it. He finishes his routine and turns to her hopefully

Rachel No, Mr Purvis.

Purvis No?

Rachel No. It's not suitable. Really. Edward wouldn't like it; I know he wouldn't.

Purvis If he saw it in action ...

Rachel No, I don't think he can be persuaded on this. He's very much a traditionalist.

Purvis (*disappointed*) Oh.

Rachel And I have to say, I'm not sure myself it would be entirely appropriate. One or two hymns, in some circumstances and some locations, perhaps. But not across the board, I feel sure.

Purvis People will be disappointed. We've been practising.

Rachel What?

Purvis There was quite a lot of enthusiasm for it.

Rachel Well, don't you think you should've asked before you launched into this?

Purvis The committee approved, and I tried to tell Edward but I could never catch him.

Rachel How many people? How many have been practising?

Purvis I don't know. About twenty.

Rachel Twenty!

Purvis Actually we thought we'd give Edward a bit of a surprise for his first service back.

Rachel No, don't, please don't.

Purvis It would make a nice welcome. At the end, you see, they all snap their hymnbooks shut and it sounds like a salute ... Like this ...

Rachel You don't have to demonstrate ...

Purvis No, I can show you what I mean. (*He takes a hymn book, opens it and waves it about as he goes into the end of the routine to the tune of "He Who Would Valiant Be"*)

Rachel (*trying to intervene*) No, I said don't, please ...

As Purvis reaches the end of the verse and is about to snap the book shut, Rachel tries to relieve Purvis of the book

Purvis (*singing*) " ... His first avowed intent, to be a pilgrim."

Purvis shuts the book on Rachel's bandaged thumb. She screams. There is a silence. She's bent double for a moment

(*Eventually*) Dear oh dear. Here, let me have a look at it.
Rachel (*quickly*) Don't touch it, don't touch it ...
Purvis You poor old thing. (*Beat*) Was that me?

Rachel looks sharply up at Purvis

I am sorry. Unfortunate timing.

Rachel says nothing. It makes Purvis a little nervous

You know, just as I closed the book ... I don't suppose we could manage that again in a month of Sundays.
Rachel (*darkly*) You don't think so?
Purvis Not with that level of coincidence.
Rachel (*with increasing menace*) I'm sure if anyone could do it, Mr Purvis, it would be you. So will you please just take my word for it? Edward won't like it. In fact, he'll hate it. I know he will.
Purvis Oh. (*Beat*) Well, perhaps just tell him from us ...
Rachel (*angrily*) No, I'd rather not, thank you. I'd rather not tell him anything. Whatever it is. I've had rather a lot of running messages backwards and forwards between the pair of you. You seem to think that's the entire point of my existence. That and taking the blame.
Purvis Oh dear, oh dear ...
Rachel Well, yes, Mr Purvis. Oh dear, oh bloody dear, as you say. And I have to tiptoe around, trying not to upset Edward, making sure I don't hurt your feelings ...
Purvis Don't worry about me ...

Rachel No?

Purvis I just don't like to see you upset.

Rachel Well, good, because that makes it a lot easier to tell you what I have to tell you.

Purvis Oh?

Rachel That you are no longer wanted here. My latest message from Edward.

Purvis (*stunned*) What?

Rachel Thank you and goodbye. Edward would like you to go. Because it's not the building that's at fault, and it's not Mrs Armitage with her ghastly, sodding banana cake, or anything else. It's you.

Purvis Me?

Rachel You, Mr Purvis. You are clumsy, you are awkward, you are a danger to life and limb, and you haven't got the faintest idea, have you? You blunder about, crashing into precious objects and setting traps for people, and you actually think you're helping. Well, I'm sorry but I can't stand it any more, so will you please, please, stop being our Health and Safety Officer before you bring the whole church tumbling about our ears!

Silence. Her anger has suddenly burnt out. Purvis is devastated

(*Quietly*) I'm awfully sorry. I didn't mean to put it like that.

Purvis No, no ... (*Pause*) Erm, perhaps I'd better just ... (*He edges towards the door*)

Rachel No, don't go, Mr Purvis. I shouldn't have said that ...

Purvis I'm sure you should. Long ago, probably. (*He looks at her a moment, turns and walks into the flower arrangement. He wrestles with it a moment and steadies it*)

Purvis exits quietly

Rachel hangs her head

Music

Black-out

The same. About a fortnight later

Some order has been restored to the vestry but Purvis's tray of face paints remains. Rachel's bag is on the table

The Lights come up and the music fades. Rachel is busy putting the finishing touches to the tidying. She's nimble and intent until she finds the face paints. She stops for a moment to remember

Purvis appears. He has his cardigan and cap on again. Rachel looks up and is shocked to see him

Rachel Mr Purvis!

Purvis It's all right. I haven't touched anything.

Rachel Where've you been? I've been trying to find you.

Purvis I went away. I thought it best.

Rachel I kept phoning. I went round to the house a couple of times.

Purvis I stayed with my daughter for a while. (*Beat*) I wasn't planning to come back, actually.

Rachel Oh, Mr Purvis ...

Purvis Then I thought that probably wasn't very fair.

Rachel There was no need. There was no need to go in the first place.

Purvis Oh there was, Rachel. I don't think I misread the message.

Rachel There wasn't a message, not really ...

Purvis "You are a walking disaster. Please leave."

Rachel I didn't mean it like that ...

Purvis I think you did.

Rachel It was just me, Mr Purvis, getting it wrong. What I really meant to say was it's perhaps not the best combination — you and safety measures. But I overstated the case ...

Purvis You said what you meant.

Rachel No, I wasn't thinking properly; my thumb was hurting ...

Purvis Yes, because I trapped it in a hymnbook ...

Rachel It wasn't that ...

Purvis Having already flattened it against the step with a hammer.

Rachel No, please. I overreacted. Things were getting on top of me at the time, and I wasn't handling it very well, and I took it all out on you. I spoke to Edward about it. I told him it was my fault ...

Purvis Well, it wasn't. Look, this is why I've come back: to explain. I was a bit stung at first, I admit, but the more I thought about it ... Well, what you said was right, all of it. I am a disaster.

Rachel No ...

Purvis I don't mean to be, but I am. I'm a blinking albatross.

Rachel Oh, please don't. I'm feeling so wretched about this. You put your heart and soul into that job — everyone at St Peter's knows that — and I was so spiteful and ungrateful about it.

Purvis It's not spiteful if it's the truth, is it? And Mary would've said the same, if she'd been here. She would've told me.

Rachel She wouldn't have been so horribly rude, though, would she?

Purvis No, probably not.

Rachel There you are, you see. I was awful ...

Purvis Well, the truth is painful sometimes, Rachel, but it can also set you free. I never realized it before but I must've been like this most of my life.

Rachel You're not like this, you mustn't think you are ...

Purvis Of course I am. This is me, Rachel, exactly me. I never really noticed before but that's probably because I had Mary trailing behind me with a mop and bucket. Putting things straight, tidying up, and most of all steering me out of harm's way. The funny thing is, I used to think she was fussing; I used to think it was just her foible — you know, tidying, clearing up, being cautious. Eighteen months without her and I've become a danger to the community. You see? I needed telling.

Pause. Purvis misses Mary for a moment

Rachel (*gently*) Really, it's not as bad as you make out. As I made out. As I said. (*Beat*) You're just a bit uncoordinated, that's all.

Purvis Uncoordinated?

Rachel Yes. It doesn't mean you have to give up. Just take a bit more care over things. Talk to people before you launch in.

Purvis I shouldn't think there's many people left to talk to.

Rachel Come on, it wasn't that bad.

Purvis No, I mean I've got the wrong side of them. Put their backs up.

Rachel That is nonsense. St Peter's has missed you.

Purvis Well, yes ...

Rachel No, I mean it. You livened the place up. Can't you see that?

Purvis With fear ——

Rachel Stop it.

Purvis Fear of personal injury.

Rachel Nonsense. You know, you're in danger of feeling sorry for yourself, Mr Purvis. You were well-liked here. Why can't you accept that? All right, a few people took a few knocks, but they were all too ready to forgive you. Honest, they were.

Purvis All of them?

Rachel I think so, yes.

Purvis Edward?

Rachel Edward?

Purvis Yes. Was he ready to forgive me? Because I sometimes felt he didn't really approve. I felt his disapproval.

Rachel No, no ...

Purvis I didn't quite fit in with his plans. You know what I mean?

Rachel Well ...

Purvis He can give that impression. He can put you on edge. (*Beat*) Does he do that to you sometimes?

Rachel Of course not.

Purvis You never get the feeling you've disappointed him some-how?

Pause. She can't answer, or look at him

I'm sorry. I'm speaking out of turn.

Rachel I've never said any of this. I don't know where this has come from all of a sudden.

Purvis No, I know. I shouldn't've said.

Rachel No, I don't think you should.

Purvis He's a good man, Edward. Well-intentioned.

Rachel Exactly. You can ask anyone ...

Purvis But to be perfectly honest, I'm not sure he's good enough
for ——

Rachel (*cutting in*) I don't think you ought to say any more.

Purvis No. Probably not.

Rachel Anyway, you've got Edward entirely wrong. He was
annoyed about the way things had gone, it's true, and he did feel
it was his duty to do something about it for the sake of the
community.

Purvis Of course. You have to care for your flock.

Rachel Yes.

Purvis Especially if you've got the human equivalent of anthrax
hanging about.

Rachel Mr Purvis, please. I'm trying to explain. Edward identified
a problem, and that's why he asked me to have a word. Which I
did. Only I really overreacted and I said some terrible things and
I was terribly upset about it afterwards. So, of course, I went to
Edward and I told him what had happened. I can do that, you
know. And he did listen. He's very fair-minded. I explained what
the job meant to you and how hurtful I'd been and everything and
how some of those things that went wrong were genuine accidents
and no-one was to blame ...

Purvis What did he say?

Rachel What?

Purvis Did he pass judgement?

Rachel He didn't actually say anything at the time, no. But he did
go to his study to think it all through. He placed it before the Lord.
And then he wrote a letter.

Purvis Edward did?

Rachel Yes, of course.

Purvis He thought about it and he wrote you a letter?

Rachel No, you. He wrote to you. So — you see? He really did
listen. I was going to put it through your door but I didn't like to.
I knew what you were feeling so I wanted to hand it to you
personally. I owed you that. (*She takes an envelope from her bag
and holds it out to Purvis*) Here you are, Mr Purvis.

Purvis looks at the envelope a moment. Then takes it

You don't have to take my word for it. You really are wanted here at St Peter's.

Purvis opens the envelope and looks at the letter

Purvis He wants me to go.

Rachel There's no problem that won't have some kind of a … He what?

Purvis He says it would be better for all concerned if I made a fresh start somewhere else.

Rachel (*snatching the letter*) He can't. He told me … He more or less implied …

Purvis It's not just the accidents, he says. I'm an unfortunate influence.

Rachel That doesn't make sense. An unfortunate influence? You? Who on?

Purvis Everyone. You.

Rachel That's ridiculous.

Purvis (*pointing to the letter*) See for yourself. It's what he thinks.

Rachel Oh, Edward. How could you?

Purvis I know I was responsible for a lot of things going wrong, but how could I influence anyone? I'm not the sort. Do you believe it? That I've been an unfortunate influence?

Rachel Of course not.

Purvis I got you cooking for him.

Rachel Of course you did.

Purvis You don't call that an unfortunate influence, do you?

There is a slight pause

Rachel No.

Purvis What do you mean? It was all right, wasn't it?

Rachel Yes.

Purvis Rachel.

Rachel Well, it wasn't perfect …

Purvis Oh no.

Rachel I probably missed something out. Or put something in by mistake. I mean, no-one could say that was your fault ...

Purvis He's right, then. I am a bad influence. I got you to poison him ...

Rachel There were a lot of gastricky things going about then anyway. We don't know it was the fishcakes.

Purvis No, it was me. Not the fishcakes, but me ...

Rachel No, listen, he doesn't even mention fishcakes. Listen. (*Reading*) "Rachel has always been easily influenced ... " (*Looking up*) You see: nothing about food. (*Reading*) " ... and she has a tendency to be rather silly and flippant at times and I believe your influence ... (*she pauses, suddenly aware of what she's reading*) ... has encouraged this tendency."

Pause. She's stunned

Purvis I don't think you were supposed to see that.

Rachel No, I think you're right.

Beat; Rachel feels about four years old

Purvis He's not mentioned it before, then? To you. I mean?

Rachel About being flippant? Yes. Yes, he has. We've had a little chat about it, yes.

Purvis Oh well ...

Rachel Please don't say, "That's all right, then," because actually it isn't. I had no idea he was planning to share it with anyone else.

Purvis No.

Rachel That is so unfair.

Purvis Yes. I mean, I don't think you're ——

Rachel I'm not talking about being flippant. I'm talking about trust. Perhaps I am basically silly. I don't know ...

Purvis No, you're not ...

Rachel But that's not the point, is it?

Purvis I don't know. I probably ought to leave, though. Leave this church, I mean.

Rachel I might just come with you, Mr Purvis.

Purvis I'm sorry. I should've taken that away to read.

Rachel I'll tell you what annoys me. He is so absolutely sure about everything. The shadow of doubt never passes over Edward. We live in the perpetual glare of his certainty, and occasionally, just occasionally, I get a little tired of it. Perhaps that's what's turned me into such an air-headed clown.

Purvis He didn't actually say that ...

Rachel Maybe we *should* go somewhere else, Mr Purvis. Set up as a double act somewhere — you tripping over things and me laughing like a drain.

Purvis (*trying to make a joke of it*) Demolition our speciality, eh?

Rachel (*still intent*) It's all so tight-arsed. I'm sorry to say that because I know it's rude but that is Edward to an absolute "T". Absolutely clenched. You could take the tops off beer bottles. (*Pause*) I'm sorry.

Purvis No, really ...

Rachel You see, there I go again. I put up with things and I put up with things, and then I go too far. Far too far. I didn't really mean all that.

Purvis Of course not. Still. I probably should go. Go away, I mean. It'll make things easier all round.

Rachel I suppose so, yes.

Purvis I don't want Edward frogmarching me down the aisle, do I? That wouldn't look very good.

Rachel Oh no, he wouldn't do that. Anyway, if we dug our heels in, there's not a lot he could do about it ...

Purvis No.

Rachel No. Except complain. (*Beat*) I'm not actually suggesting ...

Purvis Good heavens, no.

Rachel I'm only saying, we could, if we wanted, dig our heels in.

Purvis Yes. (*Beat*) Anyway, look, let's have a cup of tea. Cheer ourselves up.

Rachel I can't.

Purvis Course you can.

Rachel No, I mean the kettle.

Purvis Oh, yes, I'm sorry. Well, just cheer up, then. Put a smile on your face, eh?

Rachel tries, weakly

> Better than that. (*He takes a lipstick from the tray and hands it to her*) Go on then. Use that. It's a start, at least.

Rachel does nothing. Purvis takes another lipstick from the tray and gently applies a smile to her face with it. She lets him

> Not bad. You could do better yourself, though.

Rachel Could I?
Purvis You could.
Rachel If I dug my heels in.
Purvis Exactly.

Rachel takes her lipstick and applies a smile to Purvis's face. He then adds to the effect he's created on her face. She adds more detail to Purvis's face. They step back and look at each other. They smile

Music

Black-out

FURNITURE AND PROPERTY LIST

SCENE 1

On stage: Notice-board covered with rotas and coloured stickers
Rack. *On it*: choir and clergy vestments
Table. *On it*: church paraphernalia including box files, hymn
    books, candlesticks
Chair
Bin

Personal: **Rachel**: handbag
Purvis: fifty pence piece

SCENE 2

Re-set: Everything on table moved elsewhere

Set: *On table*: tallish vase and piles of greenery

Off stage: Checklist (**Rachel**)
Clipboard and pen (**Purvis**)

SCENE 3

Re-set: Return everything to table
Make notice-board crooked

Set: *On table*: more clutter, plus: plastic bag containing piratical
black beard and joke teeth; small tray of make-up, face
paints, talcum powder, pots of hair gel etc; roll of paper
towel

Off stage: Items to pin on notice-board (**Rachel**)

SCENE 4

Set: Board (painted with "Mind the Step" and an arrow) and pole,
                  hammer and nails for **Purvis**
                  More clutter, on chair as well as table

SCENE 5

Re-set: More signs of disorder

Set: Flower arrangement on a stand

Personal: **Rachel**: postcard

SCENE 6

Re-set: Restore some order to the vestry

Set: *In* **Rachel**'*s bag*: envelope containing letter

LIGHTING PLOT

Practical fittings required: nil
One interior. The same throughout

Scene 1

To open: General interior lighting

| *Cue* 1 | **Rachel**'s smile fades. Music
Black-out | (Page 6) |

Scene 2

To open: General interior lighting

| *Cue* 2 | **Rachel** exits. Music
Black-out | (Page 11) |

Scene 3

To open: General interior lighting

| *Cue* 3 | **Rachel**: "Don't worry about that." Music
Black-out | (Page 16) |

Scene 4

To open: General interior lighting

| *Cue* 4 | **Purvis** and **Rachel** exit. Music
Black-out | (Page 23) |

Scene 5

To open: General interior lighting

Cue 5   **Rachel** hangs her head. Music   (Page 30)
           Black-out

Scene 6

To open: General interior lighting

Cue 6   **Rachel** and **Purvis** smile. Music   (Page 38)
           Black-out

EFFECTS PLOT

Printed by The Kingfisher Press, London NW10 7AS